Lockdown-21

Bhavin Shastri

First Published in 2020

Becomeshakespeare.com

Wordit Content Design & Editing Services Pvt Ltd
119-123, 1st floor, Building No. J2, Wadala East,
Wadala Truck Terminal, Mumbai, Maharashtra 400037,
India. T: +91 8080226699

ISBN - 978-93-90040-94-0

And the beginning...

Oh my Master,

The one who resides within me.

I, Bhavin Shastri, extend my gratitude to the omnipresent strength I have found in depths of my being. This universal presence is a force behind all that arrived as thoughts and experiences and I was inspired to pen them down.

Driven and guided by all the discourses that I have heard and all the books that I could read by the phenomenal philosopher, Osho, I am grateful to them as they helped me evolve as a witness of life.

I have tried to explain my journey of Isolation during lockdown through this book.

I am thankful to each one I have met in my journey for their valuable contribution in my evolution. I owe them all, what I am.

****

Before we begin, it is important to congratulate the Prime Minister of Nation, Mr. Narendra Damodar Das Modi for his far sightedness and decision making.

Lockdown was the best decision considering then situation of our neighbouring countries.

I extend the warmest gratitude for the state of Isolation that led me to explore the spiritual quest.

We thank Mr. PM for all his efforts for creating mass awareness and motivation.

Prologue

"He, the observer in the book realizes that death is not when you die physically or you stop breathing. In true sense death was as many times he had a realization in his journey, first time when he saw the end standing in front of him, Isolated him could hear his chaotic breath. From facing the fear to getting along with it in complete surrender was the accomplishment of his journey. The way gradually he comes out to live his life further as a witness makes him an aware man. Nonetheless, the journey continues.

This book, Lockdown 21, is a voyage of each one of us who have lived the outbreak of COVID-19, this book is an opening for those who have a propensity to explore the truth.

This is about the inner churning and spiritual endeavor of each and every individual who are able to see an opportunity in crisis and finally discover them.

Lockdown-21
-----Me to Messiah

When your thoughts are hued by fear, you are sightless to find sustenance then the Journey of self-reliance start.

When we see the real state of human coinciding with a deep rooted dread and we realize that we are merely a witness to the happenings, we wake up. When we recognize our helplessness and vulnerability, we try to look for support. This support in such situation is our faith, faith in a system, power or supreme power, in whatever constitution, we try to hold it.

There has been a long standing debate between a man's faith and his blind faith. Faith is an affirmed confidence in something and blind faith is having complete trust in someone or something without any reason to do so, without even knowing it. Source of both are our belief system. So here we are talking about the feelings of belief, belief that is supported by facts, figures and incidents. However, at the same time blind faith is persuaded by convictions. In both the cases, one thing is common; it's ultimately a man's view that supports him.

Views and opinion of man is an outcome of the environment he lives in and the concepts he has been imparted by the parents and others while growing up.

Surprisingly, a man who discovers and nurtures his beliefs and notions, faith and blind faith, he only starts depending upon them.

But, what happens when both our faith and blind faith stand void. Our belief and devotion, both fail to pacify our fear and anxiety, then?

Nothing much, we understand that both were the different sides of a same coin and we find our thoughts being silent, we see the beliefs swaying and we start unlearning what we considered or knew as truth throughout. For this realization to happen, a man requires something big. Something very big to shatter him in tiny pieces, a tremor that shakes his foundation, that is the time when he becomes a watcher. Scared, worried and tired, he now starts returning to himself as he understands that either of things was empowered by him else they did not have their own existence. They were nourished by man himself to support his approach.

In that stillness of thoughts, if we pay attention, we find a call for awakening and from here the new man takes place and the journey inside begins. Man encounters his fear and starts finding ways within him.

What is a Man's biggest fear? Ask yourselves this question. What is the most dreadful thing that you can think of? The answer for all of us is common. It is the fear of end, death. Since a man is born, he knows that he is going to die, but he only knows it, never believes it.

Today, humankind is standing in a position where we all, in masses are facing this reality. We are witnessing lives end, we are watching people suffer in pain and discomfort due to the ailment and the whole world is on the verge of breaking down. Now, there is no difference between the powerful nations and weaker countries. Just a couple of months back they were the proud possessors of nuclear weapons for power display, however, today they all have a battle for survival. They are all handicapped by something unpredictable.

In this Impediment, underlying is the scope of opportune occurrence. Let's find out, what is hidden.

Day-20-The Messiah

I found you when I was lost,

Or did you hold me on watching me exhaust??

Often sinking in Ocean,

Time and again seized in sand spout

Drizzling rains or blood in my veins

You are like relief for pains.

Glimpse of you is so pure

In your eyes, I find the cure

Oh my Messiah, you accept my vulnerability

I cherish your presence with dignity

Who are you? They ask me.

I tell them he is mine, within me.

This journey of awakening, he started alone or may be it began only because of him. Yes, today it is very important that we introduce you to the one who has made it all so simple. The Messiah.

In this whole period of lockdown, although there has been lot of emphasis on isolation, but it is very important today that he makes a confession.

He has never been alone all these days, in fact he was alone before this isolation period, among the crowd, he was always alone, which he realizes now. Every one generally is, they just do not recognize, unless they find this one source of radiance.

Yes this Messiah is an illumination. He feels blinded due to the array of light when he faces his Messiah, but gradually this light leads him to darker places inside him. He sees his darkest sides, for this Messiah says that unless you see them and recognize them, how you will overcome them.

He was sweltering inside him, and he was not even aware, and this magician arrives as a dewdrop. He reaches right to the source of this burning and softly the drops fall on fire. Surprisingly, those tiny little droplets win over the heat.

He hears him clearly, feels him around, and sees him watching him. He talks to him as if he was talking to himself, or to a mirror.

Concealed within him, were lots memories and remembrances which gradually had taken shape of uncounted pains. The world is fair in those terms, happiness cannot say, but sorrows have fair distribution and we all have our own shares. The messiah caresses the wounds like a morning breeze, although at times it is like the storm of desert.

Earlier, these storms were unbearable, made him feel like a nomad, wanderer, he felt like a homeless, but later he realized that where was the home required only. The place where you live physically are your residential address, home was where Messiah was guiding him to.

The Messiah made him feel the pains more vigorously to eliminate them right from the source. This was how he was setting him free.

This whole thing was a process, the leap in him, to introduce him to the curious child hidden inside. The Messiah was firm with this child to lead him in necessary direction. He gradually exposes this child to the real quest of life and finally lets him find answers for his questions to support his growth. Who is the Messiah?

In this entire journey, he kept hiding about this occurrence in his life, may be waiting for the right time.

Finally it was the time for him to disclose the twitchy self of him. Now let's know the Messiah as per him. He says:

And thus there was a beginning of love affair-
A journey from Me to Messiah

Background: There was a declaration on a National TV; the country was undergoing something terrible. They called it a lockdown. We were hearing few new words often these days, it was one of them. It did not seem to be very difficult to stay home for few days at that time. Was it?

Day:1
It was just the beginning

With a ring of alarm, as a routine, we wake up. A man thinks he does, strange. But it was a different day; it really had a wake-up call hidden. The point is when were we to come out of our inertia? It was beginning of a higher evolution.

Well, it was alright to be at home that day. The thought was somewhat relaxing too that we did not have timelines or deadlines. That you could be in your comfortable attires for the whole day, you do not have to shave and get ready.

One could enjoy his mug of coffee without any hustle, read the newspaper, Oh no!!! Not the newspaper. Papers were to be avoided. They said that virus lived for 12 hours on the paper. Television was the better option, but what? No, it was ridiculous; all the news channels spoke about the rising figures, deaths, sufferings and helplessness. The things appeared scarier. But, what was next?

Here, we need to stop. Till a day back, we were getting the updates from media and social media about this precarious organism and its ruthless conduct but they did not bother us the way the updates did today. What was the reason? The situation was already bad around the world for couple of months. The condition was worsening as the counts of death were growing in numbers. This global threat was widening its size; however, we were not much affected.

Other days we were occupied in our routine, and we found the threat standing away. Today suddenly we realized that the end had reached us. It was standing right outside the door.

My goodness, we felt the goose bumps, the body acted to its primal instinct. Death is not an easy task to accept. No matters how well aware you are, still you will be moved on the knock of it.

Watching towards the road standing against window, the sight was disturbing. Hollowness is always cryptic; it is not something we are used to of seeing in our day to day life. No trace of vehicle on otherwise crowded road said that something was frightening.

Silence on the road and inside the house was similar: dark and dense.

Of course, by now the thought of this widespread pandemic corona virus had started entering into our heads.

First few hours of the day passed in connecting with almost all the long lost friends and relatives, mind it, long lost. These were the people he had not spoken to in many years. The question is, why today he suddenly tried what he had not done in years?

In this moment of fear, man tries to find a temporary escape. A man understands that enthusiasm, happiness and positive attitude are contagious; they can spread, although he generally is not a carrier of them. Today, he became one.

On pausing, you will realize that it was your restlessness that made you find ways to distract your thoughts.

We are fearful to even acknowledge our thoughts of being skeptical about the "tomorrow." May be because we did not know whether we are going to have one or not. Unfortunately, fear too is contagion, and it spreads very fast. This day, who so ever you might have reached to, everyone would have given an affirmation to your dread as everyone was in the same state.

Day ago, the priorities were something else, a man was planning for future, savings, medi-claims, retirement plans, however, suddenly today there was no future. Only important thought was to survive at that moment.

Although, as it was a change, on the first day, it was something different, hence it was not very bad. The change is always exciting and thrilling. It was natural to have mixed feelings on that day. However, this motionlessness life just in one day had started uncovering all the weaknesses of a man. A man starts to find it difficult to face himself. Being with self hence, remains the most complicated task. We have always been sharing, blues or bliss as we say, we share sorrows, it lessens and if we share happiness they increase. We always were in folks for everything, now that, we are isolated we are able to hear ourselves.

For now, friendship with self was not easy at all.

<u>Day:2</u>
<u>Opportunity in crisis</u>

Great adversity opens greater opportunities, and great opportunities lead to higher evolution.
– Bhavin Shastri

The fear has started taking over him, controlling him. There is no purpose as such to wake up in the morning, however, at the same time he already had an anxious and sleepless night, so he wanted to get off the bed. He feels drowning and suffocated with the rush of vague thoughts. It seemed that the lockdown is only for people, not for feelings. There was a stampede going on, on a mental and emotional level. He starts trying to find some source to depend upon, some foundation to feel safe and secure upon.

Generally in such situation man turns towards the almighty, the God. Question is not whether he ever trusted the supreme powers or not. The question remains is, what else is the option?

When a man starts thinking beyond his materialistic priorities, he gets an opportunity to think on other avenues. Today standing at the verge of end, a man realizes that his total belief system was null and void. An atheist may think of this situation as a result of the wrong deeds and karmas, and that we are paying for. He feels guilty and angry as well as he blames the medical system and tries to find fault in authorities. Whereas a believer feels that the God is going to fix it. In every way, we divert our worries and just try to impose liability on others and expect them to pull us out of the situation. This whole shift of thought process is an outcome of the panic. But what if gradually we find nothing working?

Such situation is a preparation for human's greater change.

Rampant distress then urges a helpless man to find his answers with in him as now there is no way to look for them outside. The real journey starts, the journey of quest, the journey of surrender and ultimately the self-realization. However, before that, he has a lot to go through. The process is identifying, questioning and cleansing is to begin.

****

****

Sipping his favourite ginger tea, he was aimlessly scrolling his phone. He comes across a post on a friend's social media wall which was about a daily wage earner. This picture depicted a scene where the man was sitting in terrible state, statement on it said, what are we doing for them? Certainly now as there was complete lockdown, they had no avenue to earn their livelihood. May be this man in that picture was worried for the next meal that was essential for survival.

How strange, today everyone was equally worried for the same reason, Life.

We have been hearing a lot about nature's balancing act these days. When a man interferes in the natural state of things and disturbs its course, the nature acts for equilibrium. For an example, man cuts trees, disrupts mountains and hills for his convenience, as a result he sees life threatening events like earthquake, tsunami, volcanic explosions etc.

This again seemed to be a balancing act of nature to him. He starts thinking, how we always talk about equality, and an equal distribution of wealth, opportunities and freedom. Well, with conditions applied. We talk of equality depending on individual's social stature, qualifications and physical abilities.

Now, this was the time to experience the perfect balance. No matters where you lived, what was your financial strength, whatever position you held, the threat was same for everyone.

The celebrities, political leaders, a common middle class man or a labourer, we all were living in same state of fear. Every one grounded at the same ladder. No sense of supremacy had any substance. The fear of End was ultimately playing a role of a mentor and an equalizer.

This situation for the first time appeared as an opportunity for rational thinking. The inner journey started moving towards a direction for him.

It was an opportunity in the crisis for people around the world to start observing their thoughts.

Day-3
Uncertainty puts forth everything that is important

Doorbell rings, there was a visitor and the thought froze him. He thinks of ignoring, but the bell rings again. He walks finally to open, however, 10 feet felt to be like 1000 miles. He opens the door, there was a watchman of the society, and he wanted him to acknowledge a notice that said that the management had fixed up certain time limit for elevators to function. This initiative was to control the unnecessary movement of people, especially children.

He takes a sigh of relief and appreciates the management's decision.

****

****

And the question arises, what was the reason of this fear? It was strange, how come a door bell could be a reason of one's discomfort and terror. Gradually fear of dying has started to rule over us. We are petrified of having to meet people, due to the virus. We have become the puppets and this fear is making us dance on its tips.

This was a time for clarity on some more aspects. A man has always been said to be a social animal. We survive in communities. We have social boundaries and responsibilities for which we need company and companions. The thought of being alone never gave us happiness. But this time of isolation has taught us something unexpected.

We feel safe and secure when we are alone, so ultimately it is correctly said by philosopher and spiritual thinkers that "solitude is bliss!!!You, ultimately travel alone". Oh, the moment of realization. Ultimately, it is you who matters, not that you lose compassion, not that you are uncaring, you are just helping yourself.

A week back, friends were essential, going out for movies or dining out was your ultimate fun. Today, it is all unworkable.

Today when we stand uncertain about our future, unsure about forthcoming days, our thoughts are clearer and we are able to read ourselves. We know nothing else is as important as our life.

****

****

He had read it somewhere, that incase if you are able to hold your breath for 10 seconds after taking a deep breath in. You do not have the virus in you. In these 3 days, he has practiced it for several times. Out of which, few times he could not, although he is aware that it was because of panic, still he re-tried, unless something from within gave him temporary assurance that he was alright.

The idea of meeting someone at his doorstep seemed as a suicide to him. He was aware that there were chances that he will be taken alone, kept isolated in the hospital when none of his dear ones will be with him. If things work, he may be back to him and others, if they did not he will be on his final journey all alone.

$$**$$

$$*************$$

Today as nothing seems to be as important as saving your life, we are happily alone. This isolation, another word that we hear often these days, is a tool to protect ourselves and by doing so we are contributing in war against pandemic.

This inner journey, we have started is helping us work on our unfitting thoughts. We are, only if we are, then anything else makes any difference.

<u>Day-4</u>
<u>In the times of Existential crisis</u>

The golden chance has knocked every individual. Although the journey of consciousness has started for everyone trapped in this situation, however, there are only few who will understand the actual prospect hidden in this. In these defining moments of life, day by day we come close to our own being. Isolation is another most heard and used term these days. This term again makes us opportune to spend time with ourselves. We are here in this world for some reasons. This time of emergency is a jolt for the whole humanity to find that.

****

****

He wakes up sweating badly, breathing heavy almost gasping for air, shivering and impatient. He was not sure whether he was sleeping or hallucinating. Pouring water for himself in a glass, he was able to see all his movements precisely, physical as well as emotional movements. He had found himself amid flames of fire, fenced at an unfamiliar place. He tries hard to escape but the moment he would try to step out; the fires would expand to hold him back. He finds himself fiery; he fanatically calls for help, however, there was no one. As louder he cries for assistance, the blazes rise higher. As harder he tries to escape, he feels more heat around him. Finally he closes his eyes and gives up. That very moment he comes out of the nightmare. What was the message hidden in this?

He starts connecting and evaluating the vision that he had experienced. On one hand the fear of dying, on the other hand the daily struggle of silence and loneliness, the journey inside was not easy, and yet just 4th day, he had started giving up. He wanted emission from the battle inside.

Had it been in a man's control, he would have certainly reversed the calendar to have the old days back. When life was simple, yet he made it complicated. He would have now appreciated the grace he had been showered with by the universe. He had lots of opportunities to be grateful; however, he missed on all of them, considering them, his achievements to be the result of his own efforts.

Today, as a man is silent within him, he is able to see that it was all someone else's plan and he was just the part of it.

May be the hidden message was that it is time for surrender and let the creator take its call.

Day-5
Understanding the call

With all this going on, in these 4 days, it had been a real turbulent time. A responsive man starts thinking on things that otherwise did not bother him.

Now it has become essential to understand the purpose of one's life and reason of his being into this world. As a human is born with brain; he can think and understand things. We now know that the nature is wise and systematic. This disastrous situation is not a miss of nature, It has a strong purpose may be for awakening of human.

Very rightly said by Bhavin Shastri, 'destruction needs better planning than construction.' Nature is presently in destructive mode, however, It's a creator, so must have some hidden plans.

In this time of existential crisis, when on the one hand, he was disturbed with his urge to unfold his quest; he was facing lots of distractions too. Social media playing an active role these days, right from informative news to various online events were playing as interruptions in his otherwise alert mind.

He came across a quarantine diet and fitness regime on the media platform, he has seen lots of motivational quotations and videos suggesting to stay positive on the media, every time he had a question, why is this still important for people?

Gradually he started losing interest in talking to his friends and relatives over the phone because no one could understand his state of mind and neither could he connect with their's.

He wondered that how was it possible that most of us were still untouched with the circumstances around. How was it possible that an artist was still performing the same art? A singer was still trying to establish his identity more strongly. A dancer was still dancing and trying to keep people around entertained. Was this all, at all required at this time?

He thought, if they are still into the same mindset as they were earlier then they have not understood the whole play.

An artist is not an artist only as he performs and presents certain skill. Today, understanding the real and better opportunity also is a skill, and that makes you an artist in true sense.

Now it was the time for true isolation for him. Uninterested in any external source of hindrances, he knew it was important to discover himself in this journey. He felt standing alone, however, that was alright till the time it could open doors wider for him and he could dive in self. He probably had decoded the signal or might have found someone to guide him.

He has felt the realm of emotions and thoughts, he has seen himself crumbled. Changing meaning of life and its purpose, the cultivating pursuit seemed to have preparing him for transformation. Although, sometimes he was distracted, however, his quest stood stronger than all other things.

The way circumstances were taking shape, the story seemed somewhat similar to the life of Gautama Buddha, yes before this it was just a story for many, including him that he had read and heard in parts when he was growing up.

Day- 6
When you stop, the real journey begins

When a man has nowhere to go, he then takes that leap and moves towards inside. Then the actual journey begins. This ride that we all have started in this dreadful situation can be a voyage of self. When everything else goes on a halt, Interaction with self begins. But when it starts, the actual movement happens.

****

Utterly frustrated with the chaos happening inside him, he plans to sit and pay attention to his thought. He was trembling in fear at the moment and could not find anything to cling upon. As an individual, he was disturbed with the news of sufferings and ailments around him. With every incident of death from any corner of world, he found himself tearing into pieces. He tries to understand the mystery of life.

Now, if he had not been in this condition of isolation, he would have probably never thought of this aspect so deeply.

Trying to control his rapid breathing, he closes his eyes and sits silently. Suddenly, he heard a voice "STOP". He anxiously opens his eyes, there was no one, no source of the sound that he heard, could be found.

This voice reminded him of his childhood days, in school years he had read a story of a dacoit Angulimala and he remembers, that "Gautama Buddha says to Angulimala, I have stopped long ago, When will you stop?"

This pleasant memory takes him to the life story of the Gautama Buddha.

Born as a prince, who was to become a king and a ruler, his awakening changed the entire journey of this prince turned Monk. A King without his throne, yet a ruler of entire humanity.

****

Let's now look at the journey of transformation From Siddhartha to Gautama Buddha.

Born in the kingdom of Kapilvastu, Siddhartha, a prince who lived between all possible luxuries, who was trained to rule the world with skills like archery and swordsmanship, was destined to something else. Sage Asita visited the palace on knowing about birth of Siddhartha. He met the king, father of the new born and then expressed the desire to see the child. The sage was filled with compassion, love and respect as he could foresee the future. Sage Asita started crying on a glance of the bundle of peace. The King, Shuddhodhan asked for the reason and then Sage explained that this child was to find the real meaning of life. However, as he was already old, would not survive to see it all, said Sage Asita to father of Siddhartha. He said that his tears were a mix of joy and feeling of loss. He also added that Siddhartha may choose a different path being influenced by glimpse of sufferings, which concerned the king.

Within the boundaries of palace, Siddhartha was brought up with an idea to keep him away from the sorrows.

One day when he was out on tour of his kingdom, he sees an old man, and then he asks his charioteer, Channa, whether everyone gets old? The charioteer replies, yes. He goes further and sees a sick, and the curious prince again asks his charioteer, that was he going to be sick ever? On which Channa again answers, yes saying that everyone catches disease or feels helpless at one or the other time in life. Proceeding further, he sees group of people carrying a corpse to the Shamshana to perform the last rites of a dead. By then Siddhartha was completely unaware of the vital reality of life, death. To his question about it, his charioteer replies that everyone who is born is entitled to die. This sight of pain, suffering and illness made him utterly sad. Nothing in his life till now had prepared him for this reality.

He could not rest after this incident. That day was like a thunderbolt for Siddhartha, call for making of Buddha. He decided to leave his palace and family. By then Siddhartha had a wife and a son. Leaving them all behind might have been a tough decision. However, he bids goodbye to both of them and his father when they were asleep and leaves the palace in midnight. He had lived in all possible comfort till then; roaming around in forest with a bhiksha patra must have been the challenging act at that time.

****

****

As it is said, "If you learn from your own experience, that's your wisdom, you learn from observing others, that's a skill". Buddha could learn.

Today we all are in a similar situation-We have an opportunity to awaken to Buddhahood.

Harsh realities of the end, sufferings in front of us and chances for Buddhahood are also equal for all. Yes there can be many Buddha who will encounter themselves during these days of lockdown, however, attainment is a process. Buddha also required time, he tried finding different gurus and he meditated, surrendered completely. He gradually reached to the verge of dying.

This crisis can be considered as an arrangement made for us by the nature to provide with an equal opportunity of attainment for everyone. Just that we have to start the journey, inside. Fear appears till the time we have not realized the Buddhahood in us.

Buddha's realization was exemplary. His journey teaches dropping, dropping everything along with the desire of accomplishment.

Gautama Buddha found isolation as bliss for his journey of attainment. He went into the forest and lived rest of his life finding the real self. He practiced social distancing then also. Buddha's last message for human is "Appo Deepo Bhav"- "Be the light unto you". You only need yourself in the journey

This whole incident of social distancing can be seen as a conspiracy in favour of mankind. To stop is not really stopping; in fact it is speeding up your chances of elevation.

****

****

Witnessing suffering and death for once, Siddhartha woke up and his journey of Buddhahood started. We, in this crisis are seeing the terrible things around us every now and then. Millions of people by now have died worldwide, and sitting at home we have an access to the news. Are we going to wake up to realize the futility of human existence? Will we have the awakening call now? Nature has brought tremendous opportunity for us. Distancing with others, may bring us closer to self.

Day-7-Shiva- An ultimate example of social distancing

This period of lockdown is here to remind us about the social distancing. May be we never heard about it generally, we always preached about "Stay united, we win", for the first time we were in a situation where the victory was hidden in "staying away" from people. Maintaining gap amongst each other was the need of hour. In Indian Society, social distancing was not a new concept. If we try to understand it, right from the times since human existed; we will find the traces of Social Distancing. Although the reasons are different today, however, the result can be same, awakening.

****

****

He had heaps of muddled thoughts due to the loneliness. He always felt a kind of chatter inside him. As he was engrossed into the journey of Gautama Buddha the other day, he is still thinking about his teachings. The most important of all at that time was "Appo deepo bhav", that said that a man does not need a Guru or a mentor for realization. You can self-practice and find your vocation purpose.

Sitting alone, he could see immense darkness inside him, yet he did not know the reason, however, he by now had accepted this phase. These days, it was such that there were lots of discussions about the social distancing, hence he starts finding about it. In process of understanding, he remembered the stories from mythologies, the Rishis and yogis.

When he reaches to Yogi, he has a glimpse in front of eyes; his closed eyes could see lord Shiva, sitting silently, in meditative posture. In this visualization, The Mahadev, lord of lords had calmness and serenity on his face.

He opens his eyes, and thoughts gallop, the adi-yogi, the first meditator, the omnipresent energy, Shiva always practiced social distancing. Isolation happened to be his permanent state.

Another image of Shiva flashes from memories, he might have seen it somewhere, in that picture Shiva and Shakti were in the same body, Ardhnarishwar. What did this remembrance have to say?

He again starts brainstorming, trying to find a clue, he interprets that may be this picture said that an individual is a complete identity all by himself. May be Shiva represents, that you lose yourself when in crowd and find yourself in your aloneness.

A day back, someone told him that he was slipping into depression due to the negative thoughts; they call it sadism when you do not wish to indulge into unnecessary and pointless conversations, it seems peculiar.

He now had an answer to it, although he wishes to venture into self.

****

****

Lord Shiva, the first meditator as per Hinduism is a representation of social distancing. He was a loner, a hermit (tyagi) who expounds, that inner journey is possible only in solitude. The creator, the destructor, the facilitator, Shiva is a source of life which is in inclusion of death. If you try to understand it in another way, Shiva never left anyone, nor did anything touch him ever. He had a family, yet he was alone and blissful in his aloneness. A symbol of supreme consciousness, Shiva is a guiding force for the ones seeking truth.

'Shiva is for all, none for Shiva-A Mysterious loner'-Bhavin Shastri

Shiva is a part of every being, yet he does not belong to anyone.

The half open 3rd eye of Shiva is a symbol of inner eye, a symbol of awakening. The eye that can see the nature of one's existence, we can achieve this state of awareness, however, for the process one needs to accept the approach of isolation.

Everyone who is in the inner journey needs to understand the importance of this key factor, called Social Distancing. As per the laws of Nature, human is born alone and dies alone; however, in their journey they crowd themselves with innumerable relationships, friendships and acquaintances.

Now this pandemic can be seen as an opportunity to discover the pleasure of aloneness. Social distancing may end being blissful. A human is born with potentials to become Shiva; however, the irony is that he is unaware of it.

Shiva and Shav are same. In a glance of Shiva, one can see the life and death together, creation and destruction together. He holds poison in his neck and source of life, Ganga on his head, jata. Shiva is a blend of whole energy, purity, strength and spirituality.

To discover the truth one needs to be patient and calm with self.

Day-8
Journey of a week

The journey of last 7 days have been like a roller coaster ride. For someone leading a normal life, who never paid attention to the nature and it's acts, it was a very tough time as today he was able to hear the question standing rigid in front of him.

 The one who never thought much about the cycle of life and death; to face the hardest reality right in front was nothing less than end itself. In these few days, many a times we have found ourselves standing face to face with the end of world.

There were many trips and turns that we have seen in these few days. From ignoring the seriousness of situation to understanding and accepting the problem, it has been a transition phase. From the desperation to leave the house and going out, meeting the friends to realizing that it was not worth and wise, a man has grown within him.

We have felt those scary chills in our bones and goose bumps in our gut with every incident of horrific suffering. We have felt loneliness and suffocation in the same breath.

But surprisingly, between all this, we could find an opportunity, although not everyone would, those who did, for them it was no more an end. It was a new beginning rather.

What a beautiful experience it was that one could pay attention to the inner call, and the search. Amazingly, now this wise man did not need a friend.

'Out of my desperation for company while passing through loneliness, I finally befriend myself'.

Whatever instance ensues, if it does not gain your attention and does not force you to think, if it does not navigate your thoughts, how severe the incident is, it will just come and go, it will not make any change in you and you lose the opportunity.

A man needs churning to happen and in this mixing there are chance that there would be piles of thoughts and emotions that a man will come across to. Those could bring you happiness or sorrows, memories and remembrances of mistakes and wrong doings. If you recognize your slips, then is the chance of revolution. No one exists in the world that has never made mistakes nor has no miss-deeds, but by realizing them, you grow.

As we have discussed about Shiva here, we have discussed about the brainstorming and decoding our thoughts, let's talk about churning. It is important to know about Samudra manthan, one of the holy episodes of churning mentioned in Hindu philosophy.

Once Devas and Asuras had a battle in which devas were defeated, hence the asuras took over the control of universe. To deal with the asuras diplomatically, the churning of Celestial ocean of milk-Ksheer sagar, was planned by devas.

 Here this Ksheer sagar is your own thought and the current situation we are in is the churning rod which then was Mandara parvat.

In this churning, devas on one hand found nectar, amrit for immortality, on the other hand halahal's poison too, which could have destroyed the whole creation. The Devas then approached lord Shiva, and the savior Mahadev, consumed whole poison to protect the three worlds. He held the poison in throat which in the process gave a blue hue to his throat and thus he is known as Neel Kanth.

In this process of self-reliance, we may have to become Shiva, keeping the negativity within and processing the positivity. If you reach to that stage of acceptance, you are on the ultimate path of transformation.

These twenty one days, for sure were going to unfold many mysteries. The way, we got to see that the isolation was not complex or Buddhahood did not belong to one single person, we were going to unfold the truth deeper day by day. We were on the way to embrace spirituality gradually. We were the travellers, explorers and the mentors, all by ourselves.

With all this, these thoughts going on, he finds his next questions.

-If the one we seek in outer world is within us, then why does not a man realize it sooner in life?

-While there is no so called God to be found outside, then why do we have so many institutions dividing human under different religions?

-Ultimately, what is a religion?

It was certainly not an easy task to leave the childhood beliefs and faith behind altogether and to proceed further. A man requires liberation from his contradiction.

Day-9-Nature and watcher

Now the transformation is no more an activity, it has become a process. It is happening moment to moment as now the man has an ability to see things in different manner. His approach has changed towards things and he does not simply crib over the circumstances. He has started to think rationally over the occurrences, without getting much involved in them. As today he is in process to become an observer, he is in a better position to see the difficulties and opportunities.

It is very important for a human to understand that the universe we see outside, we have the similar universe inside us too, which we realize, when we start watching ourselves. Today when we are into this state of isolation we are spending time with ourselves, we may see that in to this whole universe, we are a smaller molecule, and at the same time, inside us we have the whole universe and to establish this, nature gave us a capacity to recreate or reproduce. The inner journey plays very important role here. Now, we have a clear vision about the natural process of balance as we are able to observe the whole scenario as an observer. In this spiritual journey, that has begun, we have become more compassionate towards every being and see them all as a conception. In our silence we have seen the creator and creation, the entire cycle within us.

****

****

He was watching the television and saw some news related to COVID-19, they were talking about some trials of vaccination. Surprisingly, despite of over bragging about the achievements, the science has yet not found a solution of this problem. It is the prime concern and the necessity of the hour. Human is needed to be immunized with the virus to be protected by the virus. How strange was it? The enemy itself was a saviour too.

We do not realize that as many viruses we come across, somewhere or the other, the human body is home to most of them. There are innumerable such bugs living inside the body for our benefit, to save our lives. All the vaccines that a child is exposed to basically, is the exposure to the antigens produced from those bacteria and viruses by various processes. After the vaccine, human body gets familiar to those antigens and as a part of our immune response it starts producing antibodies to counteract those specific viruses and we start fighting the deadly diseases and become resistant to them.

Suddenly he feels compassionate and the thought emerges that if it is all created by the nature, then why is it required to destroy that creation.

As it is a threat for survival of a mankind, hence, scientific researchers are going to control the destruction happening worldwide. But their accomplishments would be again planned by the nature and will arrive to them when it is the time.

Is the science working against the nature? Is it ever possible? Basically, what we need to understand here is that nature has an antidote of all its devastations. The nature gave us virus, it has to develop immunity also for it, as of course the environment is wise enough and would not let its own creation be destroyed easily. Yes, may let it shatter. This is just the balancing act of nature to make us understand that no matters how strong we feel we are, the nature will always remain mysterious and one cannot win over the one that is unknown.

The inventions that happen in all the fields are already present in nature, although the scientists have been inventing them, however, a man has a potential only to discover them, and he cannot create them.

This pandemic can be seen as nature's reverse action on man's intentions of destruction. Now the nature has taken the control and power back to nullify the malign motives.

Human is blessed with superior qualities and powers. He has a capacity to analyze and investigate, in fact only human has a potential to invent, but what does he do with all that he has been graced with. Today whole world is together in search of medicines and antidote for the deadly virus, however, just a few months back, human was busy creating weapons for deadly affairs. We invented so many of them that every single man could die multiple times, however, when it comes to saving the lives, today we do not have an answer to it.

We kept on assembling advance weapon to fight the wars in greed of power and to establish our control over the world, ignoring the fact that the aftermath of all the battles till date say that no one actually wins at the battle field, we only lose the fights.

Despite of being the most exceptional and distinctive creation, a human keeps on planning damages, so finally the man is reminded of his limitations in various ways. With a massive earthquake or a pandemic, nature takes her call and finds suitable ways. We will surely have the required invention again to overcome this war like crisis, however, only when we come to an accord with nature in its process of cleansing.

Man forgets that extremes are dangerous, we need active scientific research and technical upgradations which is true, but at the same time, we need ultimate balance too; else no development is always a sign of progress. Nature created the war, where now whole world is struggling to get through it, the parameters; we considered being sign progress stand invalid today.

****

****

This phase is such an example of the strength of nature and limitations of human. This can be seen as a reminder for a man to understand this whole format of Middle way preached by Gautama Buddha.

The moment man will lose his balance; it will be automatically restored by nature. Like today what is the need of war, the whole world has tasted notable defeat.

On the spiritual journey, if man is able to evaluate himself, he gets to evaluate things more clearly, as he has started watching inwards, he clearly sees two similar phenomena moving inside and outside.

There are various examples around us, and we see them when we start paying attention, a person who relishes sweets and craves for it too much, forgetting the consequences, the universe inside starts sending signals. The person starts falling sick and requires to eliminate sweets to lead healthier life further. This is the balancing act of nature that's inside our body.

Similarly, man had become so destructive that the nature had to cleanse itself to create a balance. Exactly the way, if we have an organ failure, we look forward for removal and then transplantation. This whole episode is a cleansing process. But to accept and realize this is not easy. Only an awaken man in his solitude finds this whole act logical.

The way medical science has set the risk parameters for the body cholesterol, sugar, blood pressure, nature has its own parameters and the body and the environment, both, if cross those limits, they require an intervention.

Man as a watcher sees this all happening sitting across the corner.

Stirring his thoughts, he tries to switch on the television to have a quick glance of the news. However, he could not focus as had lots of questions. He finds his head spinning. Let's see what answers he gets, and who answers them?

Day-10- Revealing the sight – Quenching the quest, finding answers to his questions, he reaches to the limits beyond expectations

Q. What is life?

Answer by the Messiah

The question itself is wrong. There is nothing like life. A man lives in illusion of living his entire span of lifetime; however, a human has not left any meaning to life. Yes, if we start talking about death first, we may understand what life is, yet its meaning may differ from person to person depending upon their journey.

A man has no value for life. He has never been appreciative for what he has been receiving without even asking for. May be if man knew the value of life, he would start feeling grateful for every moment. He will start praying and extending gratitude. A man has always lived in misery; he had always been cribbing due to his negative attitude, his thanklessness. What does he crib for is even more interesting, he cribs for the most futile things, artificial to be more precise.

Due to his lack of awareness about his unsound desires and greed, man forgets to live and starts surviving, thus life loses its meaning. May be life was the most virtuous gift and man was created to be the most pragmatic bearer of it, however, he ruined it. In order to make life more comfortable, achieving more bench marks, creating more wealth, the man made his life a parcel. Now he is just busy making it little heavier to be passed on. Life has become worthless because we have lost the main ingredient of life. Celebration, celebration of each breath that you have been gifted with is the most important ingredient of life. There is a beautiful story, maybe we are aware of it as the same has been mentioned earlier too about a master and his disciple.

"This Master was an aware man, very peaceful and calm. He never got angry, had no greed, no attachment. He was always seen happy and content. He was compassionate towards all living and non-living beings. Seeing that the disciple started doubting his master as it was impossible for him to accept the peace of master as his basic trait. Finally one day he, the disciple went to his master and confessed his suspicion. He told the master that he felt that his master was faking his calm. The master on that says, 'hold on, and let me see your face first'. After 2 minutes the master says, now you can continue your question. By then the disciple had forgotten about his master and was worried about himself and he requests the master to tell him, what his observation was. Initially the master denies but later as the disciple insists, he reveals that the disciple was going to die in another 48 hours. The saddened disciple immediately leaves and reaches home. Those 48 hours, he behaves as if he was not the same person. All his tantrums dropped, he was compassionate and loving towards everyone, he apologized to everyone he thought he should. His family was in complete state of surprise looking at this change in him. As he was approaching to the time of death said by his master, he goes to meet him. On seeing him, the master asks him what he did in these hours. Disciple shares that he was a changed person after knowing about his death, and then the Master reveals, that what he had known a day prior, master had known it for years. He was aware that one day he was going to die. Hence the way, thought of death could change the disciple, awareness of it had changed the master's approach towards life and as the master wanted his disciple to understand the pleasure of being alive and letting others live, he had created a story".

The story says that you enjoy and respect the life more once you realize the holiness of death and once you start appreciating the gift of life, you learn the joy of giving. "Sharing what is more" that's the real ecstasy and meaning of life. The whole universe, rivers, mountains, trees are the form of life created by Nature. If all these give you happiness and pleasure, ultimately you start spreading life force, you love flower and you start planting more plants, you sow the seeds and patiently wait for them to germinate and bloom.

Ultimately this COVID-19 is doing the same thing. It is bringing you closer to death so that you revive the meaning of life.

The point is life and death, both treat everyone same, they do not discriminate in humans. From beginning to the end, life and death are the two different angles of same possibility a man is gifted with. Once you start loving the things as they are, you start living your life instead of surviving. Life is ultimately the journey towards end.

In a whole, meaning of life is exploring yourself, starting from you to end at you and in between finding what you are seeking in outside world, within you. Then you achieve the salvation, which is inside you.

Q. We are aware that Gautama Buddha left his palace, we have discussed about Shiva and his practice of Social Distancing. We see that today few of us are on the path of inner journey; we have started thinking in a different way. Is it impossible for a man to attain Buddhahood while leading a normal life? Your views.

Answers Messiah

There cannot be a thumb rule suitable for all about seeking and awakening.

Well, tell me one thing, before this outbreak of COVID-19, did you ever have this question. Forget the outbreak, before lockdown, did you ever thought of spending time with self. You will have your answer. In case you did, it is possible, if you did not, it still may be possible but chances are low.

Although, each one of us are born with the potential to attain Buddhahood, but there are really few to whom it happens. Yes undoubtedly, you will find many who would talk about spirituality, who would claim to know the truth, but attainment is not an easy thing. It takes a journey, lots of churning, lots of brainstorming to ultimately be at peace with self. Yet, I would not say that it is not possible that you awaken while driving your vehicle, or may be while preparing coffee for your friend, but for sure that will be rarest of the rare. Under some circumstances, this rare person would have had some journey.

Your question takes us to the life incident of Gautama Buddha. After leaving his palace; it took him 6 years to achieve his quest. In between, he searched for Gurus, he meditated, practiced extremes of self-mortification. He practiced self-discipline by ignoring desires, appetite etc. However, later he realized that he needed to survive in bodily form to attain what he was seeking. Later he chose the Middle way-path of moderation. The story says that after enlightenment, he gave his first sermon in Sarnath. As per Buddha's teachings there is a separate path for NIRVANA.

As Buddha used to travel with his Sangha, once he goes back to his Palace. On his arrival, Yashodhara sends their son Rahul, she herself does not meet him first as she believed that if she had attained some virtue, lord would certainly meet her. And it is said that Buddha did visit her and appreciated her for her sacrifice and patience. That day, Yashodhara asks him that was not it possible for him to attain what he did while still staying at home, to which Buddha does not disagree.

Now coming back to us, how much is it possible for you to stay neutral with things happening around. Is it possible for a man to drop all his behaviours, individuality and emotion easily in a present day scenario? Can a man drop his competitive attitude, his greed, and his attachments? If yes, certainly one may attain while being in the society as that would not matter to him. Point is being aware of your choices and opportunities. Buddhahood is a state meant for everyone. But then coming and going will continue.

Day-11
And questions continue

Q. It happens that an aware man, a person with exceptional awareness and positivity is surrounded with people who cling on him for strength and to escape from their negative state. Does it cause any trouble?

Answer

A negative state? What is a negative state? It is just a difference of perspective. What may appear negative to you could be someone else's entire journey. Experiences the person might have earned while crossing through their life. The point we need to understand is that we need all the energies for proper functioning. Yes, they need to be channelized. We all use battery as a power supply for electronic devices. When a battery supplies electric power, its positive terminal is the cathode and its negative terminal is the anode. The terminal marked negative is the source of electrons that flows through an external electric circuit to the positive terminal. Without this flow the battery is just a dead cell.

Hence, even the science says that both the forms ultimately are the energies and they complement each other.

The exceptionally aware man is the one who is neutral in his opinion, he does not see things with in the braces of negative and positive or good or bad. This man has chosen to be on the journey of being god now; he is someone beyond being human. With his awareness, now he has additional responsibility towards making the world better place for others. In fact the world is already beautiful, he just widens the vision of people around him.

Yes, this task requires lots of vitality and vigor, lots of patience, but now he is already aware of his capacities, he sees equal opportunities in others. He does not get influenced by any one's thoughts. What he does is, he gives an ear to people, a passage to vent out. This practice is really required for others to come out of their state. Whatever it is, if it takes them to misery, everyone should get an opportunity of liberation. The aware man brings that chance closer to them, they can just help them to wipe off the layer of smog people have around their thought process.

May be by hearing to them, you help them to see things clearly, or may be just by talking to them, you give a new direction to their thought pattern. That's the best thing you can do for any one. Rest the journey still remains theirs. They only have to define it, choose their doings; we can only help people to see the positivity around them. That may make them more confident.   It is important that we start dropping things and just watch them happen. We don't get involved.

Here again I will share a story of two Buddhist monks. They were travelling together to a village. They come across a river on the way, which was flooded. There was a woman standing helpless, may be worried to cross the river as it was flowing rapidly. Seeing her, one of the monk offered her help and held her hands to cross the river. All three reached to the other side, the woman extended gratitude and left. Both the monks were walking silently further on their journey. On which the first monk asks the other monk a reason of his silence, as he seemed to be in deep thought. Then he says that as a Buddhist monk they were not allowed to touch a female. Listening to that the first monk says, are you still with her? I left her long ago. This is what it all means. It is all about the opinion, nothing else. What could have been negative there, in that situation? Leaving the woman helpless, or helping her to reach her destination.

There are no negative and positive emotions or thought process. Everything that is present is there for some reason. And thus there is no affect as such till the time your outlook is healthy. That's what an aware man does. He stays unaffected.

Q. Can we have a world without religion ever?

Answers Messiah

Laughing, do you remember why dinosaurs are extinct today, the K-T extinction event? We need something like that to happen if we want a religion free world. Pray that asteroid falls on the earth again and we are destroyed or may be some mechanism happens and we forget the religion were born in. But again if man is alive, he will create another doctrine to divide people under different classifications. Few powerful will rule and dominate the weaker ones under them and they will create more leaders and further more divisions. Again there will be further discriminations and man will be a designer of the same. The temples and the churches are not the religions. Actually, religion is the man's approach.

When a child is born, he does not have a name but he has a religion, the one his ancestors belong to. In no conditions he is free to choose a religion of his choice and the whole life he follows and lives under the circumstances of that particular religion.

A man is ignorant about the fact that all the religious books which are created by man, are there to guide him right to the fact that the "God is one, the truth is one".

Since the beginning of civilization, groups are dominant. Let's go to the story of Adam and Eve, this division was of gender which was for the creation of mankind, that time, it was a requirement. Since then a man has been discriminating others based on physical, financial and regional differences. Then on top of all is religion, divided under the names of different Gods. All the religions try to prove their knowledge and power based on the egos and belief system. Religion is the identity a man associates himself with, without knowing the fundamentals of it. However, he has found escape in it. If you take it away, he will have nothing to cling upon. He will be more insecure and fearful and then there will be war of identity.

Hence for the world free of religion, we need the world completely to be destroyed, wiped out. A Krishna devotee can have equal pleasure while reading Quran, but he would not even try doing, in name of his God.

Quenching the quest, astonished, he could not gather who was answering his questions. Showing the direction, no one was physically present there. Was it his own spiritual endeavor?

Now he has the answers for few of his questions which are going to guide him in his further expedition.

Although the inner journey has started, it was important to stay connected to the updates as ultimately, it is the contemporary world all your actions and quest is effected by.

So now, let's see what next, the outer world has in its kit to serve us with. There was lots of disarray even outside.

Day-12
Religious belief or Obstinacy

There was news on the Television: Cases of Covid-19 have surfaced in several states linked to the recent religious congregation, Tablighi Markaz, organized in Delhi's Nizamuddin area. It has become a major worry for Indian officials trying to contain the Covid-19 outbreak. Meanwhile, the country's apex court says that 'fear' and 'panic' are becoming a bigger threat than the pandemic itself.

There were sudden rise in numbers of the patients and unfortunately they were the ones who were trying to spread the deadly disease more. How ridiculous was that? Man goes insane in the name of religion. The thought process behind this act gathered his attention and he started thinking how is it possible that people under any particular religious belief and influence feel that they are serving their God by putting their and other's lives at risk. How rubbish one is to think that he is going to be counted as a hero or may be their final abode will be jannat or swarg? Do we even know whether they exist or not? Is there any one to tell them that they are supposed to create one right here on earth?

This pain of sacrifice is a sadistic pleasure that they extract from such views.

This is such an immoral thought of a man that first, we think, we are going to protect our religion, second, we are fighting and sacrificing for 'my' religion and then the way it develops, it takes shape of 'I know more about my religion' and then for that we start maligning our own God, whom we created in order to protect and feed our ego state. These so called protectors of religion are the real pain in society

A man needs to understand that we are the favourite children of God, the God who is one for all, the God who is omnipresent. Alas! The one supreme is divided between thousands of name. Hindus top the chart by having 33 crores of them.

Of course may be no one in this world exists who is not moved by the death and the fear of one's end. Entire mankind on this day was going through the same turmoil. Who is a wise man in such situation? Wiser, is the man who incorporates the changes required in day to day life, as per the present scenario. Ultimately it is the question of existence. You need to exist at the first place to even live by your religion.

If a religion does not allow you to be compassionate and kind towards each other, whatever God you worship, it is just for namesake, you worship fake God of yours. Now what difference it makes whether you offer prarthna or namaz, you light the candles or chant Gurugranth Sahib; it is all same, null and void. It is all in vein if you do not possess an ability to respect each other and yourself too. Every religion preaches that, the "God is one", however, human by his own bull headedness is busy dividing their God and on top of it fighting, killing and shedding blood over it. It seems that the world would have been more beautiful if there was no religion.

The so called warriors or saviours of religion seem to have completely forgotten that the first religion is humanity, rest all follows. If we talk about the recent Tablighi incident, how fair it is to endanger innumerable lives in a situation where we already know the consequences. This is just an example, we need to understand the reason, why temples and mosques had to be closed at the first place, even before lockdown, before offices and schools. We were aware that a man is going to gather there in any situation, to fulfill their ambition to be known as believers in god, please note- it is also an ambition or else to gather some strength as we still live under the blind faith and establish places of worship as home for God. Do we really think God needs one?

Krishna in Mahabharata, the Hindu Mythology talks about "**Karmanye Vadhikaraste Ma Phaleshu Kada Chana**"

You have a right to "Karma" (actions) but never to any Fruits thereof.

The problem is that a man today is motivated by the result of his doing. Result, that is not even in his capacity. The greed to become someone more important or powerful distracts him from his deeds. Here the point is that the man does not understand what their real karmas are ought to be. We start to count the fruits first.

The Vedic ancient literature of World, Ramayan and Mahabharat are said to be the mythologies. These religious books of Hindusim are the stories based on belief, a collective myth. Bhagvad Geeta, The song of God, portion of Mahabharata, which is in form of dialogue between Arjun and his charioteer Shri Krishna at the battle field, talks about going beyond ethics and emotions to have your rights back. The question is why the Pandavas were right and Kauravas wrong? Politically, Kauravas were not wrong completely. Why Sri Krishna had to support Pandavas? Was it a question of being more right instead of right or wrong?

Why do we till date burn the effigy of Ravana? What wrong did he do? He kidnapped Sita for a revenge of his sister's insult. Was not he right as a brother? If we are to believe the mythology, despite of abduction, he never misbehaved with Sita, never tried to malign her identity, although he could have. Does not this man deserve respect instead of hatred? Should not every person have a little bit of Ravana inside them? He was an intelligent and brave man who preached about tapasya and devotion throughout his life.

The whole religion thing is a doctrine to safeguard the mischief of few strong upon the weaker and make them follow what few powerful men find right. How strong would be that religion, whose foundation itself is mythology? All the major religions are based on the illogical philosophies. How is it possible to conceive and have a child if a lady is a virgin? Jesus cannot be born of Virgin Marry. The blood line of Jesus Christ is another unresolved controversy that world has. All the organized religions are insignificant at the time or other. The religion that preaches that 'by killing, they are at least taking away all the opportunities from people of falling into hell,' why this ideology is supposed to be respected only at the first place. What's the mind-set of the people following this religion? If we talk about Islam, it was established on the foundation of bloodshed. To mark the extremes of crudity, we have a battle of Karbala fought in 680s. This battle is a milestone of sacrifice as well as bloodshed on the other hand fought to establish the supremacy between 2 groups.

We all today, of course have understood the complexity and consequences of the phase we all are in. Still if we plan to be enthused by our religious obligations then we are mistaken here. These were just the personal or institutionalized system. No religion ever guides to disrespect the gift of life. No religion preaches the heinous acts. No religion needs to be protected, by its followers. At the first place, religions were formed by humans, to group them together in numbers. In order to unite them for power and strength under a common name, the religious institutions came into existence. Then the masses under one were imparted with a common belief system, common faith. Then a god was created by the human to keep control over the group formed by instilling fear and blind faith. No religion came into existence before human did.

On this day, our Tablighi Jamat is one incident, however, a man has a capacity to make 100s of such incidents. Just to establish his powers and religiousness, every single man has a potential to create a massacre.

If this pandemic also does not wake us up, if it is still not enough for us to understand that the creator is wiser and stronger than us, what else will? This way, Isolation or social distancing is going to make a contribution for human. This quarantine has made us so alone, that a man has no option left than to be with self. Now he does not need a religion, why because he does not have to prove his strength or supremacy on others. It is the state where it's 'me with me, for me and mine'. Gradually, this 'me' also may vanish, then we will see the real HIM, with in us, away from the boundaries of religion. Hence 'isolation is not only for the body, it is not only for the mind, it is for our total being, for our transformation'.

Religion simply means the ultimate law that keeps the universe together, that keeps the universe in harmony and in accord. May be there were times, years back when a customary was decided, there could have been different reasons, however, may be what was right then and needed, was not going to be right in some other circumstances.

What we find today is, thought process of the generations are maligned and ruined for the sake of pseudo religion. Despite of the efforts of Prophet Mohammad in the establishment of Islam yet his Grandson and his family were killed in the battle of Karbala, just to prove supremacy between the two groups of same religion. Shri Krishna let the battle of Mahabharata happen, considering that may be it was the last battle being fought for righteousness , Jesus accepted crucifixion in order to establish peace and compassion, however, today's man is still fighting in the name of religion, reservation and strata of society.

Religions were established for the benefit of mankind; however, what we see is that the religions (dharma) only have ruined the human. A human is still preparing for more sacrifices and crucifixions, just a chance, and we are ready to hang. The battles we keep fighting for various reasons.

****

****

Day-13-Godliness and its prices

With all these disturbing thoughts, news updates and self-analysis, he has by now established a subtle bond with himself. He is more alert to his questions and his search continues. Although one after the other unpredictable instances was happening, however, living past 12 days, he has now established peace with self. He has learnt to watch the incidences as a watcher.

Another incident that was spread all over the television and social media was about the inhuman act of stone pelting by public on their saviours. The doctors and medical professionals were being attacked by people at few places as they were collecting samples to test for the virus.

How strange, just few days back the whole world said that why do we need temples and mosques when the Gods are in the hospitals wearing their white coats. The nation applauded for the whole medical fraternity and health care workers for their heroic contribution.

The workers of law and order and essential services sectors were also appreciated just few days back, and today it was a different case for many.

We have come across the atrocious assassination of the lineage of Prophet Mohammad, one who established the religion. His grandson Hasan was poisoned by Muwaayia and Hussain brutally killed in the battle of Karbala, for power hunger and to find the real khalifa who would precede the religion further. Shri Krishna played a charioteer for Arjun's cart during the battle of Mahabharat as per Hindu mythology. Jesus was crucified. All these major incidences allied to mankind are the representations of viciousness.

Jesus was said to be the eternal son of God. He who was sent by the God to set humans free from their sins, that Jesus Christ also had to face violence against him and was crucified finally. He, who was even declared as a God, had to go through brutality as he challenged the views of few. Jesus was killed by the humiliating method of execution which was that time reserved for runaway slaves, pirates, bandits and rebels.

So we may put it this way that even messenger of God had to pay the price for being one. People loved him, respected him and destroyed him too.

What happens to that trust a man shows one day? Why is man so impatient and fidgety? Let's not make them God and later claim their lives with our absurdity. Today, once again, we have done the same thing.

He starts dozing off while thinking and suddenly wakes up restless. He was confused of his own reaction and tries to re-collect his thoughts. In that nap, he had seen himself driving on the lonely road, he suddenly feels pain in his left hand and his whole arm starts getting numb, he starts sweating and feels difficulty in breathing. Gasping for air, he woke up, with another question, now in this situation of sickness, where is man going to go first, surely even if you find temple on the way, you will go to hospital first. If you, by chance meet with an accident, people who gather around, where would they be supposed to take or send the injured first? Which will be that place??

For an example, in that accident the person dies, than too, where will the body go first to be declared lifeless.

Now the point is that, in all such situations, where the question is of life and death, it is the hospital we look for. The gods in the white coats play the most crucial role in those critical hours. So finally the question is do we really need temples and mosques? When the birth and death, the main incidents of life requires hospitals and doctors, where is the need of religious houses?

The universe takes its call.

Right from Mohammed to Jesus, till today we have been pelting stones and beheading the ones who stood for us. The years have passed by, era changed, however, we still remain the same headstrong, reckless and impulsive. A man has crossed many milestones in terms of development; with pride we call ourselves developing nations, super powers. We have evolved in the field of science. We are trying to explore life on another planet and are venturing in the new zones every day.

However, are these only parameters of development? Advancement in technology, per capita income and standards of living, do they decide the progression of human?

Are we ever going to evolve as better human and present better way of living in a peaceful world? Are we ever going to share love and compassion with each other? The conflict that we have since the time of eternity is it going to continue the same way till infinity?

This incident of injured medical and paramedical forces sets up an example of our obstinate behavior. Yes truly, Godliness certainly comes with a price.

In last 12 days, on one hand, we have seen the glimpse of Buddha and Shiva inside us. We understand that we all are born with the potential to become one, however at the same time, we also see a rigid and fierce man still living within us. Hopefully one day we will overcome this man for our better self.

Day-14
Role of Self-control (Sanyam) in Isolation

The journey till now has been such that now the questions are clear, and answers are also visibly present with in. Now he could find the inner self guiding and participating to fulfill his search. We know that people are in a mess today, we all are on the verge of breaking down.

As the days are passing by and we are coming closer to the 21 days of lockdown, people seem to be divided in two segments, and the 3rd one is one who is watching this whole incident, observing the behavior of man. There are people who are staying in the houses and practicing social distancing, there are few whose reluctance is loud and clear.

In his conversation with himself in silence, what he gets to understand is that it is self-control (sanyam) that is playing the vital role in the life of people these days. The self-control that is driven by awareness is the only solution in this scenario, an awareness to wait, stop within you and come out of this deadly phase victorious.

'Self-control is the most significant armament, precisely, it is the only advantageous weapon for all the battles, inner or outer'-Bhavin Shastri.

The wars are not won by simply fighting, they are won by sitting silently and waiting for the right time, which is the ultimate practice of self-control for an armed force. Today we all are the armies in this war like situation, participating in right manner holds utmost importance.

Today, man is fighting with the inner enemy to maintain social distance and survive through the isolation. A man's greatest struggle is with his own desires and the fight is very long. Journey from unawareness to awareness, to recognize the reason of struggle will make him a new man.

Self-control is impossible for a man who is still unaware of present situation and feels that he has control over it.

Self-control has been prescribed as a way of living for man by many. Although the purpose could be different, approach is same.

In all the major religions we find the mention of Self-Control in different ways as a part of journey of attainment. If we talk about fasting, that too is a form of practicing the same. As per Christianity, Jesus Christ fasted for 40 days before his confrontation with shaitan after being baptized. During this period Jesus is said to refuse all his temptations laid by shaitan, in today's reference shaitan is our temptation for gatherings and outings, majorly.

Rozah in Islam is again a practice of self-control, abstaining from food, drink, smoke and sexual activity during the Islamic holy month. In Hinduism, we have innumerable mentions of fasting on various days like Ekadashi etc.

Here fasting is an example, although abstaining from food holds no major importance, self-control does, in terms of gathering strength to stay calm and peaceful with self. If human needs to preserve his desires, to achieve attainment, which today is winning the fight with self to hold on and keep going with social distancing, he needs to practice self-control. Generally, man has been found mixing patience with self-control, yes they go together, yet are different. Self-control is an activity that a man plans for betterment which is an outcome of awareness. Although patience is also derived by awareness, however, it is an emotional flow.

The only way to succeed through trials and tribulations in life is through patience, awareness and self-control.

 This Self-control is the only alternative we are left with as the virus has already grown out of control. Standing apart is a new standing together.

This phase will pass, however, this skill and its importance if we comprehend today, we will be at the better place forever. At times the impulsive actions and temptations lead a man towards unwanted results, once we understand self-control and patience we start pausing automatically.

The pause that we are imposed with today requires an inward pause too.

Day-15- Living with the foes, finding the friends

We are not fighting a physical war, we are not wrestling with an opponent, it is not the battle of flesh and blood, and still he finds himself between the struggles all the time. He finds himself amid the conflict.

Although at the surface, now things look to be little settled, within him an unknown war was going on. One after the other the confusions were dissolving and emerging. He is a person of lots of friends. He used to be a center of attraction of the parties. Witty and jolly him have been likeable to many and he had enjoyed that privilege of being people's favourite. He used to be one of the most energetic and enthusiastic participant in social events and occasions.

However, today, in this period of isolation, in the raging and troubled time, all those whom he considered to be his friends, were not making much sense to him. In fact for a moment, he found those memories to be the distraction for his present day's state. Precisely, memories of his fun trips and celebrations looked to be pulling him back from the state of awakening he was living in.

Well, he was in the state where he felt that all the social obligations and responsibilities were drifting him away from himself. But the point is that how to comprehend the genuineness of even this thought, was it a correct interpretation?

He wanted to find the reasons for this unexpected variation in his personality. His internal emotions may pull him down and external temptations will certainly not let the transformation happen easy.

****
****

Bhagwan Mahavir in his teachings says that 'there is no bigger enemy than your own greed, anger, pride, hatred and attachments, all these are the parts our own being.'

This again takes us from where we started, what we are seeking outside, is actually residing inside us and we are unaware of it.

Whether it is bliss or sadness, compassion and love, the supreme power or enemy; human is the power house and we have all the positives and negatives stored with in us.

In fact, maybe there is nothing like positive or negative, it is just the way we are looking at it.

For an example, if we are in a problem that we never dealt with earlier. We do not have a clue or way out to fight with it, we feel trapped and worried. Although, we feel that it was never going to end, however, we work hard on it, keeping patience and finding best possible solution. Finally we find ourselves out of it after lots of efforts. Now imagine the happiness, this pleasure will not be only for eliminating the trouble, whereas we will be happier for the illumination of our own personality. Once you overcome the trouble, you find yourself to be stronger, you gain experience and learning. You be more prepared.

So now, point of thought is, whether that situation was an enemy of your peace or a friend. It made you more aware, confident and widened your areas of expertise. Hence everything that seems to be problematic in the beginning is not necessary the one.

Going back to what Bhagwan Mahavir teaches, if all the negative traits he talks about are parts of a man's own personality, then why a man is unaware of his greed and his anger.

That means that he never could pay attention to his thoughts. For sure if a man starts recognizing his greed, it will vanish as no one wants to live in misery. If the man starts recognizing his anger, he will start dropping it gradually. Who wishes to spend time in anguish and annoyance?

It is important that we be free from these traits to see the real self of us and to understand the basic nature of a human, we need to accept them too. Once you stop fighting, you start setting yourself free for further growth. Man needs to become a watcher of all his emotions, he will realize that if you do not get involved, these will just come and go. They are not him; they are just part of him.

You accept love, you need to be settled with hatred too as compassion is a sweeter fruit only because brutality tasted bitter. A man arrives to the loving state when he drops fight with his emotions.

Making peace with these enemies, evolves one as a human, hence these no longer remain the man's enemy.

In this social distancing, though a man is in agony; however, this condition is bringing him closer to himself, despite of many problems. So, that's an opportunity.

After quite a long time, people have got an opportunity to stay at home for days at a stretch; they have started to value life. As a modern day human barely gets a chance to focus on his emotions, today he is able to understand that he loved the chirp of birds, breeze of wind. As he is able to value his own life, he recognizes the value of other living beings too. He is more compassionate.

On attachment, there is a story of Bhagwan Mahavir's disciple Gautama. Gautama was one of the most sincere disciples of Bhagwaan. His devotion was exemplary. He was very close to awakening, however, could not. Bhagwan knew the reason. He kept on telling Gautama that it was time for him to move further as his attachment for his master had become a constraint for the disciple. One day Gautama had gone to nearby village for some work, on his way back he got the news of Mahavir's parinirvana (death). Gautama was shattered completely, he felt as if there was nothing left for him. Then he asks the person who gave him the news, that whether his master left any message for him and on that the master's words that he had left for Gautama were, "How long will you keep on holding on the bank, when you can freely flow in the river?"

Here, Bhagwan Mahavir guided his disciple Gautam that the journey was his, and he had to walk it alone leaving all the attachments back in complete isolation.

Even if love for your master becomes an opponent for growth, you have to drop that too. This attachment comes from within so dropping must happen from inside.

The Social Distancing has taught so much. All the evils and virtues are within us hidden, within us in form of energies, and every energy is an opportunity. All the distractions are created by man, by his own thoughts. He can negate them well, if he is aware.

Ram and Ravana are equally important for evolution of mankind, and ultimately dropping both and realizing one is the eventual treat.

At the time when we are moving towards awareness and awakening, on the spiritual path in this quarantine, either we will wake up to ourselves, or else we will die as miser as we are today. It is all going to be the result of our own choices driven by our awareness, patience and self-control.

Day-16
Being one with Oneness

This period of lockdown has taught us very important lesson. A man has learnt to be content with the availabilities. In this situation, we know that the resources are limited and avenues very less. People are bond to live with what they have. What this teaches is that the requirements of a man are very less in comparison to his desires. Man has dropped his celebrated stature and has come down to the elementary lifestyle. Surprisingly, he is finding bliss in it. Although, cribs sometimes.

Now this was a materialistic approach, however, how about those who have addressed their inner call and withdrawn their fight with self. Where are they going? What is next for them?

He has stopped the self-arguments and is on the accepting end, whatever comes.

It is ultimately about unfolding you and getting along with yourself. Nothing else is important than your own being for your attainment. We all need to explore and find out our way.

****

****

Sitting in his balcony, sipping his cup of ginger tea, he was thinking how the basic cup of tea, he has started relishing. And the process started right from boiling of tea leaf. He could enjoy the refreshing aroma first, that took him to the freshness of tea garden. He could see the colour, he felt the warmth, and enjoyed the taste. He had never felt a cup of tea could give him so much of contentment.

A man keeps on arranging the luxuries and loses on the elementary happiness.

Today, the thought process itself is new; he, who never thought of end of life, now has started to accept it gracefully. He has understood that death does not arrive suddenly, it was right there since life is. He has understood that life and death are two ends of same thread, bank of the same river.

Now this was the forced situation, imposed by nature. Although, he had not chosen but gradually his silence and solitude has started finding bliss and serenity in it. This was probably the power of acceptance. Once you accept, you surrender yourself to universe, you find yourself amid gratefulness and devoutness.

****

****

He is full of gratitude at this moment as he has an opportunity to realize the beauty of simplicity. Now to him the entire thing appears as an occasion of celebration, celebration of realization, celebration of devotion and celebration of love.

The man has started believing that the one he is searching for is inside him only.

While thinking of devotion, he starts thinking of love and compassion too and now the question arises that whether these two emotions were same or different. He feels that devotion will happen only in case you feel love, whether it is for yourself as here we are talking about the self-search and if you feel devoted to someone else, than too devotion will be a stage of love and vice-versa. A way to reach to yourself, through a form which may be non-existent. We can have arguments on this; however, what is the need to prove anything.

Both, love and devotion are non-measurable as these are feelings, pure and pious. A devotee, drowning in love and a lover in complete devotion. They co-exist. Devotion is defined as a strong feeling of love and love can be explained as passionate feeling or emotion of affection, attachment, and devotion.

Love and devotion can be seen as Radha and Meera for Krishna. You really cannot make a comparison between the two, in fact, there is no comparison as they lived in different era.

Radha was the complete representation of love and delight.

On the other hand Meera's, devotion and love for her Girdhar Gopal was so intense that she left everything for him. The luxuries of life and social pressure nothing could stop her. She considered Krishna as her husband, how foolish. Who does that? Krishna did not exist in the era when Meera did. She saw a marriage procession happening in the neighbourhood, she was just a child and she told her mother that she will marry Krishna and as she grew up her child's play became so intense that she believed Krishna to be her husband.

For her, Krishna was never present physically, still she always spoke about his existence. After her marriage with Bhoj Raj Singh, elder son of Rana Sangha, ruler of Mewar, she could not begin the marital bond, saying that Krishna could only make love to her. She could surrender only to her Krishna. This was an emotion of a woman who was completely in love with this man Krishna and her devotion was such that just in his name she could consume poison and still survive. She would sleep with the idol of Krishna in her bed, and thought it was only a question of few years for her to meet him.

She poured all her sexuality, sensuality, love and devotion all to one who did not even exist when Meera bai did. What was this all mystery about? In then society, it was of course unacceptable. She was considered as a shame for her royal family, attempts were made to kill her and finally she had to leave the palace due to the pressure to lead normal life. But she had strength to go through any trouble effortlessly and that strength she gained from her love for her Krishna who she had established with in herself.

Her single-minded devotion to Lord Krishna kept on growing and she happened to reject all the societal pleasures. Self-realization that she is remembered for so reverently was the result of her devotion for her beloved that survived within her. She conversed with Krishna, she ate with Krishna, her Beloved and in the end she merged in his illumination.

What exactly was Krishna for Meera other than her beloved? Krishna was a consciousness for Meera.

Meera was clear that Krishna was the source that was going to help her towards inwards journey. Since she heard about Krishna from her grandmother, stories of Krishna gave her immense pleasure. An innocent and adorable child Meera created an image of Krishna and started sharing happiness and sorrows with it in her heart. As she grew up, she developed love for that image and ultimately she discovered her true self while dancing in complete devotion for her beloved. This was an example of Prem Bhakti marg.

Guru Nanak was also on the same marg, prem bhakti, while Meera achieved her divine self dancing, Gurunanak dev ji reached to attainment singing for his prabhu pyara, known as remembrance (sumiran) . In the end they both emerged within them and dissolved with in themselves.

Kabir kept on writing, and his writings were his way of finding self, his karma gave him pleasure and strength to stay in the journey of being one with self.

Buddha found his way in meditation, Mahavir in austerities, but ultimately the destination was finding self.

No matters what your way is, no matters what form you choose, but ultimately it is the search for self and this non-existing capacity, exists in you. You cannot find it anywhere else. Rest all your gods are just the form and methodology. Now, whether it is Krishna, Jesus or Mohammad, does not make much difference.

Had Meera been told about Mohammad or Jesus, it is possible that she could have been influenced by them and then she could have established either of them as her beloved. Now what difference does it make, ultimately it is always the search of self that you are going to find with in. Now may be you visit the temple to offer prayer every day or walk barefoot, those are your karmas that take you to the journey of exploring self, once you start exploring self, drowning within, you achieve the ultimate omnipresent, who has always been living in you.

Meera's devotion was eventually her search of self. It takes courage to believe in something that you have never seen physically, she had not seen Krishna as in existence and still she established him as a non-existential force that directed her journey. She is said to be an enlightened sant of prem bhakti marg, she had attained to the self.

This is what happens if your karmas or your worship take you to the right direction and you are aware that it is you and only you that's the universe. The one is the seeker, is the seeking, then you are one with oneness

****

****

He was mesmerized listening to the Bhajan of enthused poetess, ideal of devotion, a selfless lover and indeed a revolutionary woman.

She was indeed one of the foremost embodiments of Premabhakthi (divine love) and an inspired poetess. For sure, she might have found him within her. She felt his presence in her heart.

When Meera danced immersed in love for her Krishna, only dance remained, the dancer vanished, so did her ego. Completely lost in devotion for her beloved, she was in state of complete surrender, with no expectations and no complaints.

Meera bai lived completely absorbed in love, when she did not even had glimpse of him, yet there was no space left in between as her beloved was always within her.

She was a representation of purity, simplicity and divinity all in one. Meera and her oneness with the one unknown is certainly an unresolved mystery.

The lockdown has given us all an opportunity to find that beloved inside us. Yes he exists, yet we are unable to recognize him.

****

****

Day-17
Law of Sharing

Everyone on this earth is fascinated with the thought that he is doing extra for this world and what he gets in return is lesser in comparison to his contribution. What a strange thought? Who can give what when everything is already into the hands of someone else? We are just receiving what we deserve. What we are bestowed with, we do not have capacity to pay back for it. Why is man always indulged into calculations? Are we ever going to have non materialistic approach? It is not always give and take. We are only taking that too without realizing the importance of the virtue.

****

****

He is again today moved by something strange, a doctor couple in Italy died due to the nCOVID-19 as they were treating the patients and were exposed to the deadly virus.

Along with that many such cases were arriving across where the protectors were paying the price of being responsible and dedicated for their duties. Then we get to know of a doctor who was threatened by the neighbours just for performing her duties, saying that as she dealt with covid patients, she is a threat to the ones living around her. There were landlords who asked the residents to vacate houses as they were medical professionals.

How a human becomes so ruthless with another human? These were those people who should have been celebrated for their contribution, yet they were suffering due to our self-centeredness.

People have been bragging about the financial contributions made, but those are the materialistic things, which is still possible to give and share, that too within the limited capacities, although even that contribution cannot be ignored as we are in need financial aid to facilitate the necessities.

However, if we look around, the ones who are working tirelessly for the society, the cleaners and sanitation workers, the law and order workers, they are extending more than what they have received. They live with bare minimum resources, yet are capable to perform good for society and if we look inside us, how many of us are going to be able to donate our time and put our lives at stake.

Still surprisingly we lack gratitude towards them. We are uncomfortable sitting at home; they are fighting outside amid this fatal situation.

****

****

Have we ever thought what would happen if the nature starts taking back what it has given to us? Nature gave us flower and its fragrance together. What do we give back to the nature? This whole universe is based on the joy of giving. The day it starts taking back what the universe has given, we will end up with nothing as the life itself is a gift from nature and it can only have control over it.

Today people are ready to serve the humanity with all the possibilities, be it their health, knowledge, talent, dedication and time. We can say that they are the ones who are actually returning what they have got from the nature.

You may feel that a doctor is a doctor because of his own potential, yes he worked hard, which is not untrue; however, there is another angle to it.

Nature supported the circumstances so that they could become one.

It is very important for human to explore his potentials and expand the capacities, which indirectly lets them serve the society. The nature is always kind to maintain equality of opportunities. It instills, one or the other quality in each one of us so that we will be able to return some of what we are granted with.

This whole equation of giving or sharing is the one this world is based upon and one who deserves, he gets what he is meant for. The one, who deserved to get the final savings from Mohammad Sahib's life, got it finally.

We have a story to share here associated with the life of Prophet Mohammad, a night of his death, he had very high fever. He was impatient and restless; shivering due to the temperature he asks his wife that had she reserved something that day, because it was an unusual feeling for him.

Now, It is important that we bring our focus to very important fact of Mohammad Sahib's life, whatever he used to earn the whole day, he used to give it away by the evening. He never planned to save anything for the next day and that was his way of life.

On his question his wife replied saying just like any other wife, she was worried about her husband, and hence she had kept a little for emergency. It was midnight, yet Mohammad

Sahib, the messenger of God asks her to find someone needy and bequeath what she had. This was the man, who could not die in peace, unless he shared, whatever he had.

On that his wife says that where would she find anyone at that time as it was already late. She was insisted to go out as Prophet Mohammad said that the one, who requires, will be waiting. That very night he left his body. Mohammad sahib throughout his life followed what he preached. "Joy of giving"

Human is busy counting his wealth and his contributions. If we look at the concept of donation, it can be a means to quench the thirst of ego of a Man. We have seen it many a times that people make donations and expect a certification of same. For an example, one who contributes in building a temple wants his name to be inscribed on the walls.

These days we come across lots of news of people making huge financial contributions to aid the fight against CORONA which make us feel proud.

Such crisis situation introduce the philanthropists in many ways, may be by serving the society or by financial support.

Amidst all this, the support of the worker who contributes his life without any expectation remains unnoticed, it is strange though. Who taught these people to risk their lives, who asked the deceased doctors to accept the end of their lives for others? It was the inner sense of responsibility for few in this society who ultimately made it large by their karmas.

When we talk about sharing, we cannot forget to mention about sharing of knowledge and wisdom. A man since he is born starts learning, in various manners, now imagine how wonderful it would be if we start sharing what we have experienced in the journey. When we share, we open our heart, and if you see in larger context, when you are sharing, you are receiving too.

May be if you let the energy of sharing flow, the nature will not have to reinstate the energy.

"You miss to take care of the nature, the nature starts caring for self and if you care for nature, you surely are doing for yourself as you too are a part of it, in fact the whole nature."

Day-18
Death, the ultimate lover

You do not recognize yourself and you claim to live your life to the fullest. You say that you live for self, and you do not know who that self is. This time is to identify whether this 'self' of ours is hidden, dead or alive inside us.

It is unfortunately very common that usually we are dead when we look alive. Either we live for others or we live someone else's life unless we do not recognize the true self of us, until the revolution happens.

After the revolution, once this journey from doer to watcher happens, the actual transformation takes place. This transformation is equivalent to death, as after this the doer inside really dies. He stops doing and with that he drops his ego and accepts the happenings to be the course of nature. He starts understanding that he does not make decisions.

Death is an ultimate lover, not talking about one when the body is cremated, but when the doer dies. Once it happens, we start living as a watcher. Living every moment as an aware man.

****

****

He was analyzing how this lockdown has put the world upside down. Fighting the fear of death, we moved closer towards it.

But, we were still alive. Then what is death? Is it just the stopping of heart beat or brain waves that cease?

To him it appears that what actually is considered death is just the end of cycle of life an indication of the end of physical presence, suspension of breath.

On the spiritual path, the death happens before we die. This is the death that happens when we start moving towards ourselves.

While thinking of the life in past two weeks, he realized that there were so many illusions that were naked now.

He felt that he was the one responsible for things he did or achieved in his life, he many a times used to think that he was indispensable at his work place. His presence was precious for his family; his existence was much important and made difference to many.

As we all live in an illusion of doing things, planning and deciding, suddenly we have realized that we are nothing. We don't really have the capacity to do and plan, actually this thought of doer is also implanted in our mind by the nature.

Now he has become a witness, an aware man who just observes things the happenings, transition of day and night.

This man has a 3rd angle to everything as he sees things without being involved in them now. This is what we talk about Shiva's third eye. This half open eye is a symbol of awareness.

The moment a doer becomes a witness, that very moment is his attainment. That's the real death, liberation from the unwanted.

Being isolated in this lockdown, a man has found true essence of his life.

****

****

Now, the man has started to settle with the hurdles and hitches of lockdown. It is true that if you are in any particular situation for some time, you adjust according to it and start finding your comfort zone in that change.

But then this change is temporary, the moment situation changes, we start re-adjusting accordingly. If a man becomes spiritual due to the incident, the chances are that he will lose his pursuit as the memory fades, the change will be provisional.

Awakening is about recognizing the opportunity hidden in that particular moment or event and then leaving it behind to move further on the same journey. If the external sources change the inner us, we are still asleep, it was a temporary rousing.

Your basic foundation remains unchanged unless you skip that one breath.

'*The one breath in which you realize the worth of patience, passion, concurrences, voyage, deferment and destination, this one breath in a moment is the foundation of a new man within you'- Bhavin Shastri*

Death is when you are not the same person when you wake up next morning. Each time you realize something new, the old you dies and the new you are born. There are so many roles you play in lifetime, they all die each time you do.

Unless we dissolve multiple times, we are just consuming the breath that is counted. Living requires multiple deaths.

As we have always heard that when the soul leaves and finds a new body that is death. So here, the body remains same; the soul emerges to be more aware, which is a real celebration of life, the ultimate death.

Day-19
Life after death- The beginning of new end

Resting in my coffin, I see myself as a lover of life.

After these few weeks, when life returns to regularity, few of us will go back to the normal days. We will have stories to share of our sufferings and struggles. However, few will be the ones who will continue walking on the path they found these days, they have actually discovered their true selves, tested the nectar of peace in isolation.

Nature is kind; it will keep on reminding us of the golden chance we received to attain Buddhahood.

This course of awakening has changed a lot in him. In due time, he evolved as a human. He has seen limitless universe inside him. He has now left the way of living he had been doing for years.

During lock down, living in isolation, he has died numerous times. He was thinking about the days when the lockdown had just started. Every news of death disturbed him, he lived in fear, he screamed for freedom out of this. Addressing his anxieties and fears, subsequently he kept dissolving within himself. Although, he was still breathing but he was a different person, a livelier, and a liberated man. A better version of him.

The 'He', who on the first day of lockdown was furiously calling his relatives, has died, and he found the new 'Him' in these 19 days. He encountered the most hidden facts of himself, he was today grateful to the tremendous opportunities he had encountered these days.

<u>The self you are, you will be one</u>

<u>The one you are not, you will discover.</u>

Exactly this is what has happened with him. Travelling through himself, he has found the true self of him, which was still pure and untouched. It was like he had seen himself being peeled one after the other, dropping the layers those were whacking over him.

****

****

He was sitting silently observing the sky, it was still blue, still the clouds were scattered in patches over the infinite. He could still feel the wind and its sound, sun was equally bright, water did not seize to be cold. Music was still soothing; he still flipped his phone and has started to interact with friends and relatives. He still wants the lockdown to get over so that the things could be back to normal. The life that had come to a halt would start moving again. Mobility of a man was very important, for the earth also rotates. He wished to go out and watch a movie, although, he had already seen many characters with in himself. He had witnessed all sorts of emotions and playfulness together.

He was still worried about workplace issues, economic slowdown, recession and job losses.

When everything still was same, what good this whole spiritual wakening did to him?

****

****

Now here we need to pause. It was not about becoming someone else or something else. It is about unbecoming what one is not so that one actually becomes what one is capable of becoming. Something that one is born with possibility to become.

Nothing surely changes, nature still continues its pattern, sun rises in the east and sets in the west, what changes is the watcher. Now we do not blame nature for drought in Maharashtra, for we know it is wiser than us. We today have the capacity that in case if someone bullies us in the name of cast or religion, we smile and move away. We can enter the temple and the church just as entering into the garden or the sea beach, well as we have seen the one living there, inside us.

Sitting on the couch we have seen ourselves lying on the floor wrapped in a shroud and we were calm by the thought.

So what difference is it all? It is the awareness. Once awakening happens, you proceed to awareness and acceptance. The lesson learnt happens to be-letting go.

****

There is a Beautiful Zen story of ten bulls. This story is about the search and principle of life where a man goes to find his bull in dusk, this bull is his search. This pictorial presentation is in 10 parts that explains the spiritual awakening and its stages.

The first painting says about the beginning of search, the quest that is barely paid attention to as we are busy in other worldly affairs. Finally, one day something happens, like today we have Corona to align us to the hidden search.

The second painting depicts finding the path that is identifying the form. Any of the way that purifies you, connects you with yourself could be your form. The third painting says tasting the nectar, that first sign you realize of moving towards the right direction, the first death. But the 4th painting of this series says that it is not easy, you will try to find an escape, and the 5th painting is about the journey further, you bring yourself back, realizing that the distractions too are important as they ensure you of moving ahead. Once you are aware of your fidgety mind, you start watching its mischief, you start the journey further, says the 6th painting. 7th painting says, now you seize to fight with your mind and both start on the same journey. And then both the mind and you have vanished in the 8th painting, they transcend and find everything meaningless. Right from the beginning the search was clear, truth was one and so was the awakened witness. In the 9th painting you become a watcher who sees creation and destruction together, without indulging into them. The 10th painting says what? It says that you go on to celebrate your life and whatever you see, appears beautiful and awakened.

<u>So the awareness is that nothing is supposed to change; now I sip my coffee more aware.</u>

It is simple, after enlightenment Gautama Buddha realizes that he was hungry and he eats rice pudding. An enlightened person does not do things differently, he is just aware that he is not doing, it is being done.

The quest that started in the secret lighting to which he could not find source, has led him to his own foundation.

Who was in this journey along with him?

Day-20
Me to Messiah

Continued...

He shares the love affair in his own words.

An unknown enormous impression enters my life. He comes closer to me and initially I try to hide myself. But he is so certain to find me that he did not leave unless I face him. I was on edge of screaming in his presence. It was very disturbing. I never opened the doors, where did he enter from.

I asked him, who are you? The answer I get is 'I am your Soul'. I felt scarier. Once he was in, he did not leave. I made my attempts to elope, but where would I go as he was always watching me.

He saw my tears rolling down and ensured that he never wiped, unless I did it for myself. He gave an ear to all my questions but did not give an answer easy. He made me strive to know the meaning of my life but once I was ready, he held my hands to ensure that I move into the right direction.

When I ask about life, he tells me about death, when I ask about attainment, he talks to me about journey, I ask him about stillness, he explained about the chaos inside me , I ask him about love, he takes me to the karmas.

I yell at him, I scream at him , I get so angry that I feel like scratching his face, but then in all this waves of emotions, every time, I realize that he was guiding me towards righteousness, the correctness.

Never he replies anything straight, but ensures that I find answers for all. So, that is my Messiah. He makes me, a 'Me' instead of making me a 'HIM' and leaves me with an option to disagree, or agree with myself too.

That was the first day when I could look straight in his eyes. Those firm and stable eyes spoke about the mysterious journey of life after life.

Those eyes were the stillness I was searching for. It was clearly visible that beneath the stillness, there have been layers of anxieties, fear, anguish and disturbance. That's the day when did I realize that I could see myself in those eyes.

He, the Messiah was so inflexible and unscathed with emotions, looked as if he was not bothered of the feelings, but at the same time, he taught me the lesson of compassion towards others, towards all the living and non-living beings, towards nature. He enthuse me with gratitude and thankfulness for all that I am bestowed with. He opens up the vision for joy of giving and law of sharing, for he knows, nothing belongs to us. Not even the time and not even our breath.

He looked to remain untouched with the emotion of love, but he is the one who actually imparts the skill in me to love myself. Says 'Hug yourself'.

He does not have his sermons; he has his Geeta and Quran inside him. His way of existence in a whole is moral of life.

I was agitated to hear die before I die, for we all were struggling with the fear of death already, and he touches my heart and the death has a different meaning today. I wish that I die before it is too late. Death is the ultimate lover today, I desire for the union with it. The 'I' dies, the witness lives.

I ask him, are you mine and he says 'For me, he is mine' He accepts my tantrums and ego-trips, helping me realize them on my own, and smiles at me to keep it easy and makes me flow. May be I am a new man in making.

His calm and serene appearance fills me with lots of optimism and tranquil.

So finally who is this Messiah, he who lives inside us all, yet we never get acquainted with. The way Meera had her non-existent Krishna as form within her, I have my Messiah inside me living moment to moment. He is my beloved watching me all the time. I owe him my existence. Grateful, am I that I found HIM. Fallen in love with him, I rise in me. Magnetic force of him pulls me out of me. He was always present in me; I could not recognize him soon.

Our way of living brings us the contentment and distresses which is based on our own choices. If we choose attachments, we are to face clashes that cause sadness. A man keeps on holding back till the time he does not find a force to guide him right and that force is always inside him, his inner voice, his eternal companion. For Him that's his Messiah.

The never ending love affair with self goes on.

Day 21
Knowing the nothing

We have come across the different ways of attainment chosen by different seekers. We have come across the different karmas of them, as per the requirements of the situation.

Gautama Buddha chose meditation, Mahavir's renunciation, Meera's devotion they all found their ways, which were different from each other, but the destination was same. They were also in the search of self through the one Supreme.

In the process of seeking, the sole purpose is always finding the self.

We are fortunate enough that we have references today. We have the teachings of Jesus Christ, Mohammad Sahib, Bhagvad Geeta, Gurugranth Sahib. We have examples of philosophers and lovers, stories of their oneness and attainment. But all these are just the references. When Jesus might have arrived, he had none, neither did Mohammad sahib have. They had to find their own ways, without any examples.

Gautama Buddha chose his way which was the self- realization.

We are in search of us, not in process of becoming someone else. Whatever your idea of god is, you find in yourself, you will find him within.

No outer God is true; the truth is one that you find within yourself.

To attain Buddhahood, you have to overcome Buddha- Bhavin Shashtri.

It is very important that we keep our cups empty so that we don't miss the chance of learning or knowing. Spirituality too brings arrogance, people who have tasted are well aware. The quest will be there till the time you are not dead completely, to find the answers, is now your responsibility. If it comes naturally, accept it. It does not, drop the struggle.

But as the journey has just started, there is a long way to go. In between you will find obstacles and disruptions, but that's how the journey is supposed to be. Do not run away as there is no escape. Be there and face them, for whatever happens, it has a bigger prospect.

Life has no purpose, other than attaining what is more beautiful and serene than death, however, it should come effortlessly. Till the time we are struggling, we are still trying to do, and then the doer has to die again.

Every success has its own failures

And every failure comes with an opening for better prospect.

Desire to succeed is not worth at all- Bhavin Shastri

You need to escape from whatever comes as a hindrance on the way, do not get involved in them, escape the clouds, so that you see yourself clear.

There would be only two persons in this world ever to have lived nothingness in true sense, one to arrive first in the world and another to leave the world last. Neither desires attached nor any reference to go through.

Awareness is the state that you discover within yourself that will keep on reminding you of your journey. They both will have nothing to gain and nothing to lose.

There is a story from the life of Kabir and Farid. On request of their disciples, both of them planned to meet once. They gathered at a common place, Kabir and Farid on two different sides and their disciples on their sides. Their disciples were waiting for them to interact as it was expected to be one of insightful day, may be the disciples wanted to see the superiority.

They all kept on waiting for hours, however, either of them did not even utter a single word and yet the communication happened.

Mostly all the significant communiqué are silent. The communication with self is one of them which are the most vital one.

Kabir was one enlightened sant of prem bhakti marg who never preached about any god, who considered all the religions to be one. He taught of acceptance of all and the self, primarily. Kabir in his dohas says the fragrance that you are searching for is with in you.

We all are in a quantum revolving around in the orbit again and again, spinning in the whirlpool of feelings, but there are really few who take the leap to reach the actual state. We are born with all the possibilities to attain Buddhahood, nature has distributed all the resources equally, yet the call happens for just few.

From the array of Darkness, we fetch some light,

To guide inside through the tunnels, long and endless

Hoping that we see the other end, heart fills with gratitude

From fright to endurance to self-assurance

However, the Journey still continues.

About Bhavin Shastri

Bhavin Shastri, the author of Lock down-21 is a constant voyager in never ending quest of life, music, and discovery. He believes that every creation of nature is bestowed with the best possibilities to attain Buddhahood, provided we are ready for the spiritual revolution inside us.

"An expedition that leads a human to encounter their true self is the real journey"-Says the Author.

He is an eminent artist, who through his music spreads the magic of love and peace. Bhavin Shastri is a soul who understands human emotion and lives his life as a witness to them.

An engineer by profession, he is a musician by choice. A Sufi singer, he says that Sufism is an approach of living that is much a need of time. It is a healing force that cherishes those deprived of self-love and assurance.

'He says, an art that does not bring you salvation, is a curse'

Bhavin Shastri is honored by the title of "Shahenshah-E-Sufism" (the king of Sufi songs) in Gujarat for his magical Sufi singing, being devotion his genre.

This book is an answer by him for the seekers who are still waiting for an opportunity. Lock down-21, is his first literary venture in form of book, although he has been motivating the society by writing various spiritual and informative quotes.

He is a true patriot and his love and respect for nation are easily visible in his speeches and events. Not to forget Bhavin Shastri is a prominent contributor in social evolution and believes in law of sharing.

Bhavin Shastri is a marvelous orator who easily motivates the masses to walk that extra mile.